Registry of Guitar Tutors

ALCM
Electric Guitar
Performance Diploma
Handbook

Compiled by
Merv Young and Tony Skinner
on behalf of
Registry Of Guitar Tutors
www.RGT.org

Printed and bound in Great Britain

A CIP record for this publication is available from the British Library
ISBN: 978-1-905908-22-6

Published by Registry Publications

Registry Mews, Wilton Rd, Bexhill, Sussex, TN40 1HY

Cover photo by Michael Ruiz. Design by JAK Images.

Compiled by

Registry of Guitar Tutors
The Specialists In Guitar Education
www.RGT.org

Contents

⦿ CD track listing

Introduction

This publication is the second in a progressive series of three Diploma handbooks aimed primarily at rock and pop guitarists who wish to obtain an accredited high-level performance qualification beyond that of Grade Eight. Although the primary intention of these handbooks is to prepare candidates for the Registry Of Guitar Tutors (RGT) Performance Diplomas, the series provides a comprehensive structure that will develop the abilities of any guitarist – whether intending to take the diploma examinations or not.

Those preparing for an examination should use this handbook in conjunction with the *Syllabus for Diplomas in Electric Guitar Performance* and the *Electric Guitar Performance Diplomas Exam Information Booklet* – both freely downloadable from the RGT website: www.RGT.org

CD

A CD is supplied with this handbook both as a learning aid and also as an integral part of the examination. The CD contains examples that provide an indication of the standard of playing expected for this diploma, as well as the backing tracks that candidates will need to undertake the examination.

ALCM Outline

There are six parts to this diploma examination, each of which is briefly outlined below:

❶ **Technical Studies.** This handbook contains the notation for three unaccompanied technical studies. The examination requires the candidates to select one of these to perform.

❷ **Prepared Performances Part I – Melodic Improvisation.** The accompanying CD contains the guitar theme and backing music for three classic rock/blues tracks. The examination requires the candidate to select and perform one of these tracks with the accompanying CD and to develop and interpret the original guitar theme.

❸ **Prepared Performance Part II – Rhythm Playing.** This handbook contains the chord progressions for the three drum and bass backing tracks that are included on the accompanying CD. The examination requires the candidate to select and perform a rhythm part over one of these tracks.

❹   **Lead Improvisation.** The examination requires the candidate to perform a lead solo over a previously unseen chord progression. This handbook and the accompanying CD contain examples of the type of chord progression that will be presented.

❺   **Rhythm Improvisation.** The examination requires the candidate to improvise a rhythm part whilst following a previously unseen chord progression. This handbook and the accompanying CD contain examples of the type of chord progression that will be presented.

❻   **Chart Reading.** The examination requires the candidate to perform a notated rhythm part whilst following a previously unseen chord chart. This handbook and the accompanying CD contain examples of the type of chord chart that will be presented

Tuning

For examination purposes guitars should be tuned to Standard Concert Pitch (A=440Hz). A tuning guide is provided on the accompanying CD on Track 1. The use of the CD tuning track, an electronic tuner or other tuning aid, prior to or at the start of the examination, is permitted; candidates should be able to make any further adjustments, if required during the examination, unaided.

Other Examinations

In addition to the ALCM Performance Diploma, RGT also offers the more advanced diplomas of LLCM (Licentiate Diploma of the London College of Music) and FLCM (Fellowship Diploma of the London College of Music). A DipLCM Diploma, of a level preceding ALCM, is also available.

RGT also offers a full range of professional guitar teaching diplomas: DipLCM(TD), ALCM(TD) and LLCM(TD). A comprehensive range of pre-diploma graded exams for electric, acoustic, bass and classical guitar is also available.

Exam Information Booklets for all of these exams can be downloaded from the RGT website: www.RGT.org

---

Technical Studies

Candidates should select and perform ONE of the three unaccompanied technical studies notated in this chapter.

All of the studies are in the key of A minor and include techniques such as string bends, legato, slides, vibrato etc. Each of the studies is very different in terms of style and musical content, although each has been designed to assess a candidate's accuracy, fluency, coordination and control of the guitar.

Each study has been recorded on the accompanying CD to enable candidates to clearly hear how each one is expected to sound. Candidates are encouraged to listen to the tracks carefully to ensure that their performance is an accurate reproduction of the audio/notation.

Technical Study No. 1

This study features a combination of diatonic scale and arpeggio sequences. The study has three distinct sections, with each section requiring a different set of playing techniques.

The first section, from bars 1 to 7 inclusive, contains an eight-note legato phrase that finishes on the root note of the chord that each phrase is based around. The first phrase is based on an A minor chord and the phrases descend down the fingerboard with the final phrase being centred on B minor b5. Candidates should ensure that the eight note legato phrase is picked once only on the first note; the remaining notes should be played using hammer-ons and pull-offs. The final note in each bar is played with vibrato using the fretting hand – NOT a 'whammy bar'.

The second section, from bar 8 to 14 inclusive, contains a series of diatonic arpeggio phrases that are played using a combination of slides and string bends. This arpeggio sequence commences with A minor 7 and ascends the fingerboard until finishing with G dominant 7.

The third section, the final two bars, features a series of 16th note arpeggio figures that descend from A minor to B minor b5 before ending with an E7 and A minor chord. The final harmonic note is played by tapping onto the A string at fret 12 with a finger of the picking hand.

This study can be heard on CD track 2.

Technical Study No. 2

This lively study contains three sections that utilise a combination of legato and raking techniques, string bends, vibrato and diatonic scale sequences.

The first section, from bar 1 to 6 inclusive, features a three octave A natural minor scale that is played with a series of ascending triplets. The final bar in this section has the tonic note being played using a string bend with vibrato from the fretting hand (i.e. not using a 'whammy bar').

The second section, from bar 7 to 12 inclusive, features a series of descending unison string bends. The first three bars are played as double-stops with the pitch of the bent note being the same as the note that is simultaneously fretted on the high E string. The next three bars feature a string bend followed by a fretted note; the pitch of the bent note is the same as the pitch of the fretted note that follows it.

The third section, from bar 13 to the end, contains a diatonic octave and scale run that descends the A natural minor scale before finishing on A5 (power chord). Each scale run commences with a short percussive 'rake' being played across the strings (muted with either the fretting or picking hand) to lead into the first note.

This study can be heard on CD track 3.

Technical Study No. 3

This study focuses on a combination of string bends, legato and vibrato techniques, as well as palm muting and rakes.

The first section, up to the start of bar 7, features a series of short melodic phrases. Notice that the desired melodic effect comes from the accurate use of the notated bends, legato techniques and vibrato.

The second section, from bar 7 to 13 inclusive, is a development of the initial phrases but reproduced one octave higher. There are also some subtle technique variations that need to be followed carefully.

The third section, from bar 14 to 17 inclusive, contains a series of A natural minor scale runs using mostly palm muting with the picking hand. The first note of each bar in this section should be accented and played without the use of palm muting.

The final section, from bar 18 to the end, features a series of repeated, accented notes played with vibrato. After a 'rake' leading to a string bend with vibrato, the study finishes with a slowly strummed A minor chord.

This study can be heard on CD track 4.

Performance Tips

- You should perform your chosen study at approximately the stated tempo. Fluency and clarity are more important than speed for its own sake, and slightly slower or faster performances will be acceptable providing the tempo is maintained evenly throughout.

- There is no requirement to perform the studies from memory, nor will any additional marks be awarded if you choose to play from memory.

- You should demonstrate accurate and fluent control over the instrument at all times, in an assured and confident performance.

- You should perform your chosen study using a clean guitar sound and without the use of any additional effects other than subtle reverb if desired.

- You are required to perform your selected study exactly as indicated in the notation and without any embellishment or variation of the rhythm or pitch.

- All the notes should be picked exactly according to the notation, i.e. played with the appropriate techniques such as hammer-ons, pull-offs, slides, etc. as indicated.

- You should ensure there is no lapse in the tempo when moving from one section or phrase to another. Each study should flow smoothly throughout.

- Ideally, you should follow the fingerboard positions indicated in the tablature for each study. However, alternative fingerboard positions will be acceptable provided the pitch, accuracy and musical content of the study is not compromised.

Abbreviations used in the notation:

S	= slide
BU	= bend up (ascending string bend)
RP	= re-pick a string whilst the string is bent
BD	= bend down (allow a note to descend following a string bend)
H	= hammer-on
P	= pull-off
PM	= palm muting
L.V.	= let the note(s) ring
TH12	= tapped harmonic + fret number for the picking hand to tap
Vib ⌁	= vibrato

Technical Study No. 1

♩ = 104

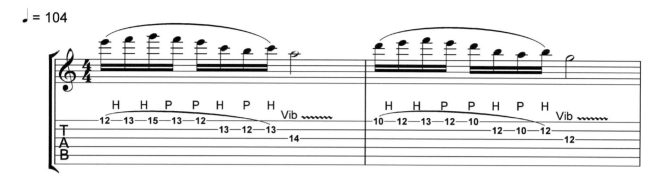

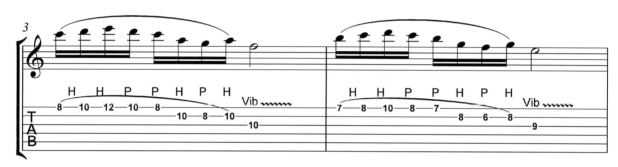

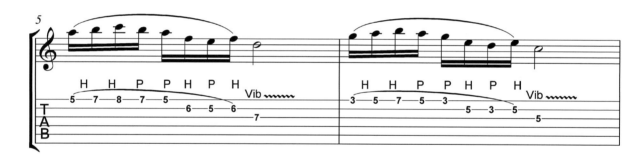

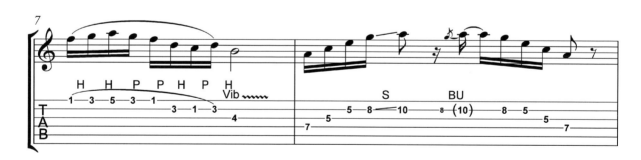

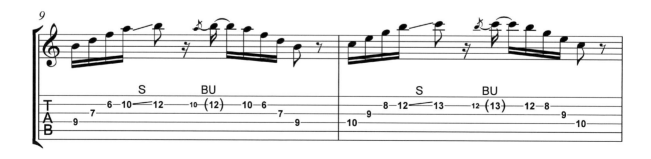

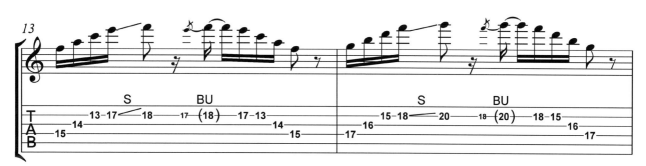

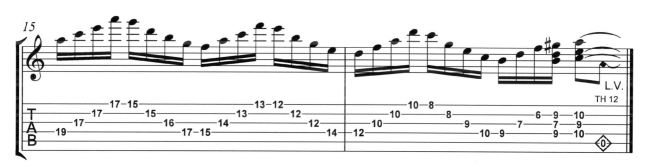

Technical Study No. 2

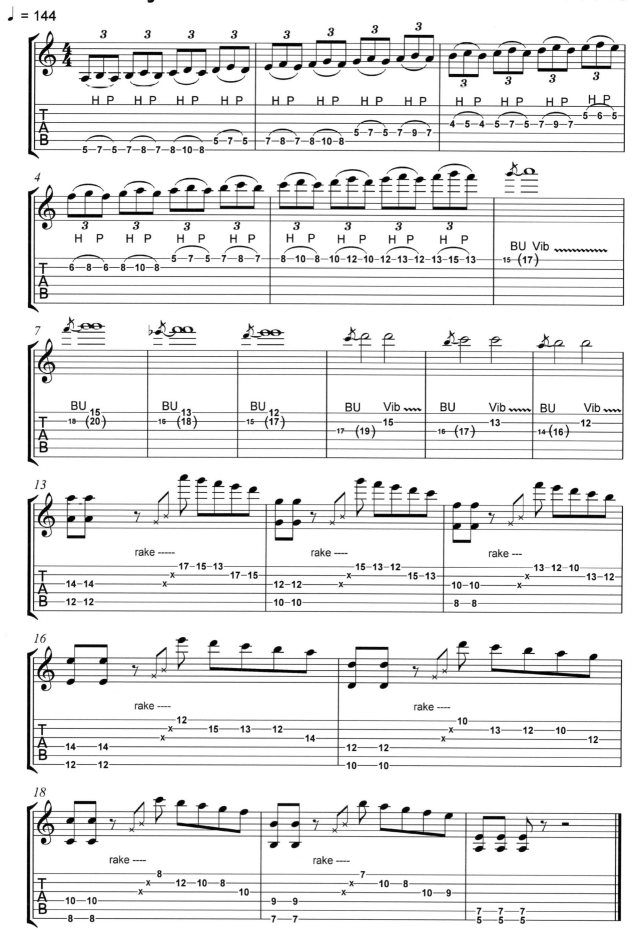

♩ = 144

Technical Study No. 3

Prepared Performances
Part I - Melodic Improvisation

The accompanying CD features three tracks containing a guitar theme and backing chords taken from the following classic rock/blues tunes:

- Need Your Love So Bad (Fleetwood Mac with Peter Green version)
- Shine On You Crazy Diamond Part 1 (Pink Floyd)
- For The Love Of God (Steve Vai)

Candidates are required to select and perform from memory ONE of these guitar themes over the accompanying backing CD. While the backing chords continue, candidates are then required to develop and interpret the original theme in a musically creative and imaginative manner that is in keeping with the style and character of the original theme.

Each CD track contains the backing chord sequence for the guitar theme played through six times in total. Over the first sequence the guitar theme itself has been recorded onto the CD for the candidate to hear. During the second sequence candidates are expected to reproduce this guitar theme *exactly* as it sounds on the pre-recorded version that appeared over the first chord sequence. During the third, fourth and fifth sequences candidates are required to develop and interpret the theme. During the sixth sequence candidates should play the original guitar theme again as an exact reproduction of the pre-recorded version. To avoid compromising the style and feel of the original, all of the tracks feature a fade-out at the end of the sixth chord sequence.

First sequence	-	Pre-recorded guitar theme (candidate listens but does NOT play).
Second sequence	-	Candidate reproduces the guitar theme.
Third sequence	-	Candidate interprets and develops the theme.
Fourth sequence	-	Candidate further develops the theme.
Fifth sequence	-	Candidate continues to develop the theme.
Sixth sequence	-	Candidate plays the original theme again.

Candidates are required to perform their chosen guitar theme from memory.

No notation has been supplied in this handbook for either the guitar themes or the accompanying chord sequences because at this level candidates are expected, as part of their exam preparation, to be able to work out and make informed, musical decisions regarding scale choices for improvising as well as fretboard and fingering choices for reproducing the original theme.

Although candidates may wish to notate the theme and/or chord sequence themselves, as an aid to learning prior to the exam, candidates will not be permitted to use, or refer to, any notation during this section of the exam.

The ability to develop and interpret the guitar theme in a way that is both musically varied and interesting but still in keeping with the essence of the original theme is fundamental to this section of the exam. Candidates should not simply perform the theme, improvise a solo that is musically detached from it and then return to the original theme; instead candidates are required to demonstrate mature and appropriate musical decisions that develop, embellish and vary the original theme.

In order to obtain a high mark for this section, candidates should demonstrate a high level of technical accomplishment and a consistently secure level of accuracy, fluency, clarity, articulation and dynamic range beyond that expected at DipLCM level. The degree of musicality will be important and playing should demonstrate a mature sense of musical style. The performance should be confident and assured and should at all times communicate a clear sense of individual interpretative skill, with a clear ability to engage the listener fully in the performance.

It is essential that you bring the CD from the book with you to the exam.
During the exam, the entire CD track you have chosen will play through without stopping. The end of the pre-recorded guitar theme should be taken as your cue to commence your performance – with the exception of Shine On You Crazy Diamond (see note below).

Need Your Love So Bad – Fleetwood Mac with Peter Green version   ◉ CD track 5

The guitar theme for this track is taken from the opening 8 bars of the song and draws mainly on the A pentatonic major scale.

Shine On You Crazy Diamond Part 1 – Pink Floyd   ◉ CD track 6

The guitar theme for this track is taken from the 6-bar section of the song that commences at approximately 5 minutes 10 seconds on the original album. This section of the song is in the key of G minor and uses the G blues, G pentatonic minor and G natural minor scales. Due to the compositional structure of the original, candidates will need to commence their reproduction of the theme just as the pre-recorded theme is coming to a close.

For The Love Of God – Steve Vai   ◉ CD track 7

The guitar theme for this track is taken from the opening 16 bars. It is in the key of E minor and is based around the E pentatonic minor and E natural minor scales.

Performance Tips

You are encouraged to listen to the original artists' recordings of the set tracks as they contain numerous examples of musical ideas that will influence and inspire your playing. As well as the studio recordings you might also wish to source some live versions to gain further insight into the techniques used by these players. However, whilst your improvisation should be stylistically appropriate, examiners are not looking for a straight 'sound-alike' reproduction of these players' solos. You are encouraged to be creative in your approach and express your individuality, whilst maintaining appropriateness to the musical genre.

Performances will probably be enhanced by incorporating a variety of appropriate techniques such as slides, string bends, vibrato, slurs etc, and where musically appropriate, you are expected to demonstrate fluency and confidence in the application of arpeggios, chromaticism and double-stops.

The melodies have been recorded with an overdriven (i.e. distorted) or a clean guitar sound depending on the track. You are, however, at liberty to use either a clean or overdriven sound for this section of the exam; any appropriate guitar effects can be used providing you can set them up promptly and unaided. The examiner is not permitted to assist with this in any way, and may ask you to proceed with the exam without the use of effect units if you are unable to set them up quickly and efficiently.

There will be a number of fretboard and fingering options available to you as you perform the theme and your variations. You are urged to explore these various options thoroughly when practising for this section of the exam. You are expected to demonstrate a creative, confident and comprehensive handling of your guitar when performing this section.

Prepared Performances
Part II - Rhythm Playing

The accompanying CD features three tracks containing a drum and bass backing track in the following styles of music:

i. Slow Blues   ii. Rock   iii. Funk

Candidates are required to select ONE of these backing tracks and perform *from memory* a rhythm part over the accompanying backing CD. Candidates are required to demonstrate musically creative and imaginative rhythm playing skills that are in keeping with the musical style of the backing track.

Each CD track commences with a two-bar count-in, followed by the drum and bass sequence played through four times in total. The track will end with the root note of the first chord in the sequence being played once.

The accompanying backing CD also contains a fourth track with a rhythm guitar part recorded. *Candidates may not select this example track to use as their rhythm playing performance piece.* This track is included purely to provide an example of the appropriate standard of playing and musicianship that is expected for this exam. It is not intended that candidates should in any way replicate the ideas on this example track in their own performances.

The ability to interpret and develop the selected chord progression in a way that is both musically varied and interesting, but still stylistically appropriate to the backing track, is fundamental to this section of the exam. Candidates are expected to demonstrate proficiency in a wide range of rhythm playing techniques and to display mature and appropriate musical decisions that both complement and enhance the drum and bass backing track.

The basic chord progressions for each backing track are presented overleaf. Candidates are also expected to use chord embellishments and extensions, where musically appropriate, to enhance the performance.

In order to obtain a high mark for this section, candidates should demonstrate a high level of technical accomplishment as well as a consistently secure level of accuracy, fluency, clarity, articulation and dynamic range beyond that expected at DipLCM level. The degree of musicality will be important and playing should demonstrate a mature sense of inventiveness and musical style. The performance should be confident and assured and should at all times communicate a clear sense of individual interpretative skill, with a clear ability to engage the listener fully in the performance.

Backing Tracks

The chord progressions for the three backing tracks are as follows:

Slow Blues

● CD track 8

♩. = 60

‖: **12/8**   A9 | D9 | A9 | A9 |

| D9 | D9 | A / Bm7 / | C#m7 / Cm7 /|

| Bm7 | E9 | A / D9 / | A / E9 / :‖
x4

Rock

● CD track 9

♩ = 152

‖: **4/4**   Dsus4 / D / | Dsus4 / D / | Csus4 / C / | Csus4 / C / |

| Dsus4 / D / | Dsus4 / D / | G Bb C F | G Bb C F |

| E7 | E7 | E7 | E7 | E7 | E7 | E7 | E7 :‖
x4

Funk

● CD track 10

♩ = 126

‖: **4/4** Gm / Cm / | Gm / F / | Gm / Cm / | Ebmaj7 / D7 / |

| Gm / Cm / | Gm / F / | Gm / Cm / | Ebmaj7 / D7 / |

| Ebmaj7 | Ebmaj7 | F | F | Ebmaj7 | Ebmaj7 | Am7b5 | D7 :‖
x4

The chord progression for the example track is as follows:

Slow Fusion Ballad

● CD track 11

♩ = 88

‖: **4/4** Em9 | Em9 | Cmaj9 | Cmaj9 |

| Em9 | Em9 | Am7 Bm7 Cmaj7 C6 |

| Dsus4 | D | Dsus4 | D7 :‖
x4

Performance Tips

It is essential that you bring the CD from the book with you to the exam. During the exam the entire CD track you have chosen will be played through without stopping; the end of the two bar count-in should be taken as your cue to commence your performance.

You are encouraged to listen to a selection of tracks from a variety of artists in the musical style you have selected to perform, i.e. blues, rock or funk. This will provide you with numerous examples of musical ideas that will influence and inspire your playing. Drawing on a wide range of ideas and influences when preparing your rhythm part will enable your performance to be creative and varied, whilst maintaining appropriateness to the musical genre.

As you are expected to demonstrate proficiency in a wide range of rhythm playing techniques, your performance will be enhanced by incorporating some of the techniques listed below, where musically appropriate:

- Different fingerboard positions of the same chord: a variety of chord voicings, including the use of open chords, barre chords and partial chords.
- Use of extended or altered chords or chord embellishments.
- A range of strumming styles.
- Plectrum and/or fingerpicking arpeggiation.
- Splitting chords between bass and treble parts.
- String-damping (both fretting-hand and strumming-hand).
- Adding single or double-note licks between chords.
- Use of double-stops such as octaves, thirds or sixths.
- Chordal slides, as well as chordal hammer-ons and pull-offs.

You are at liberty to use either a clean or distorted sound for this section of the exam. Similarly any other appropriate guitar effects can be used provided they can be set up promptly. The examiner is not permitted to assist with this in any way, and may ask you to proceed with the exam without the use of effects if you are unable to set them up quickly and efficiently.

Although chord charts have been provided for this section of the exam *you are required to perform your chosen rhythm piece from memory.* Although you may wish to notate some rhythm ideas as an aid to learning, you will not be permitted to use, or refer to, any notation for this part of the exam.

Lead Improvisation

Candidates will be presented with a previously unseen chord progression. Candidates are allowed one minute to study the progression and are then required to improvise a lead solo over the progression, which will be played by the examiner (either live or on CD).

After a one-bar count-in the chord progression will be played through five times without stopping. Candidates should not improvise during the first sequence of the chords, but rather listen and digest the tempo and style of the progression before improvising over the remaining four cycles. After the final sequence the progression will end on the first chord.

The chord progression will be in either $^4_4$ time, lasting 12 bars, or in $^{12}_8$ time, lasting 8 bars.

Candidates should produce a standard of improvisation beyond that expected at DipLCM level, demonstrating secure and versatile technique and clear evidence of a developing musical personality. Candidates should display a clear understanding of how to create an effective improvised solo that is accurate in terms of note selection, timing and phrasing in relation to the accompaniment.

Candidates are expected to demonstrate evidence of variety in their choice of scales, arpeggios and playing techniques in a fluent and musically appropriate manner. In addition, candidates should be able to demonstrate an ability to make effective use of the full range of the fingerboard. This Diploma requires an effective performance that clearly demonstrates a developing sense of interpretative skill. Candidates should demonstrate evidence of a perceptive and versatile approach to their choice and application of melodic and rhythmic ideas during their solo.

In addition, where musically appropriate, candidates are expected to be able to demonstrate a level of control over the application and execution of the following techniques that is worthy of a professional performance:

- String bending
- Vibrato
- Slurs
- Pick control

Example Chord Progressions

The following are examples of the type of chord progression candidates may be presented with in this section of the exam:

Lead Chart Example 1   ● CD track 12

$\begin{Vmatrix}:\frac{4}{4}\end{Vmatrix}$	Gm7		Ebmaj7		F		Dm7	
	Gm		Ab		Ab7		D	
	Cm / Cm7 /		Eb / Ebmaj7 /		Am7b5		D7	:‖ x5

Lead Chart Example 2   ● CD track 13

$\begin{Vmatrix}:\frac{4}{4}\end{Vmatrix}$	E		F#m		G#m		C#m	
	F#m / C#m /		A / G#m /		A		B7	
	D		D		B		B7	:‖ x5

Lead Chart Example 3   ● CD track 14

| $\begin{Vmatrix}:\frac{12}{8}\end{Vmatrix}$ | A | | E | | D / E / | | A | |
| | F#m | | C#m / F#m / | | B / B7 / | | E / E7 / | :‖ x5 |

It is important to note that the sample chord progressions provided on the previous page are supplied purely to provide examples of the *type* of chord progression that may occur in the exam. These examples are NOT the actual chord progressions that candidates will be given in the exam.

The first chord of the progression will be the key chord, so the first example shown is in the key of G minor, the second example is in the key of E major and the third example is in the key of A major. In the exam the chord progression could be in any major or minor key; the examiner will not provide any advice or guidance regarding identifying the key or the scales or playing approaches to adopt.

While the chord progression will be predominantly diatonic, up to two bars may contain non-diatonic chords. In minor keys, the V chord may be minor (or minor 7), dominant 7 or major.

Performance Tips

Your improvised solo should be musically and stylistically appropriate to the style of the rhythm guitar accompaniment. While you are expected to demonstrate clear evidence of your own individuality, you should also be able to draw upon relevant musical influences to ensure a musically appropriate performance.

Performances may be enhanced by incorporating a variety of appropriate techniques such as slides, string bends, vibrato, slurs, double-stops etc. Where musically appropriate, you are expected to demonstrate fluency and confidence in the application of arpeggios and chromaticism. You are also welcome to use a range of other playing techniques, where musically appropriate, such as sweep-picking, finger-tapping, harmonics and whammy bar. This is your lead solo and your chance to demonstrate your own particular skills.

You are at liberty to use either a clean or distorted sound for this section of the exam. Similarly any other appropriate guitar effects can be used provided you can set them up promptly and unaided. The examiner will not assist with this and may ask you to proceed with the exam without the use of effects if you are unable to set them up very quickly and efficiently.

You will be presented with a chord chart that is typical of songs from a rock, pop or blues genre. You will notice from the examples given that the chords and progressions have been deliberately kept relatively straightforward and, apart from the non-diatonic chords, are not overly complex in terms of harmonic structure or movement. This approach is designed to encourage you as the soloist to bring energy, interest and variety to the performance through your use of harmony, melody, rhythm and playing techniques.

You are expected to demonstrate versatility in your scale and arpeggio selection, although not at the expense of a fluent, melodic and confidently phrased performance. You should endeavour to demonstrate versatility, fluency and confidence in your approach to improvising your lead solo.

Rhythm Improvisation

Candidates will be presented with a previously unseen chord progression. Candidates are allowed one minute to study the progression and are then required to play the chords, improvising a rhythm part.

The chord progression will be in either $^4_4$ $^3_4$ or $^{12}_8$ time.

The range of chords presented will be restricted to the following:

- Major
- Minor
- Major, minor and dominant seventh
- Minor 7b5
- Sus 4
- Major and minor sixth
- Major, minor and dominant ninth
- Common 'slash' chords (i.e. chords with non-root bass notes)

The chord progression will be *predominantly* diatonic, although some non-diatonic chords may be included. The chord progression will be limited to keys generally used in pop and rock music.

Candidates should produce a standard of rhythm playing beyond that expected at DipLCM level, demonstrating secure and versatile technique and clear evidence of a developing musical personality. Candidates should display a clear understanding of how to create an effective improvised rhythm part that is accurate in terms of both chord selection and timing.

Candidates are expected to demonstrate evidence of variety in their choice of chord shapes and playing techniques, and to incorporate these in a fluent and musically appropriate manner. This Diploma requires an effective performance that clearly demonstrates a developing sense of interpretative skill. Candidates should demonstrate evidence of a perceptive and versatile approach to their choice and application of rhythmic ideas during their performance.

Dynamic markings have deliberately not been included in the chord charts – in order to encourage candidates to use their creativity to create their own individual interpretation in this section of the exam; the omission of dynamic markings does not in any way imply that dynamic variation should be absent from the performance.

In order to obtain a high mark for this section, candidates should demonstrate a high level of technical accomplishment as well as a consistently secure level of accuracy, fluency and clarity, and a suitably varied dynamic range. The degree of musicality will be important and playing should demonstrate a mature sense of inventiveness and musical style.

Example Chord Progressions

The following are examples of the *type* of chord progression candidates may be presented with in this section of the exam. The first example has also been included on the accompanying CD – purely to provide an example of the approximate standard of playing and musicianship that is expected for a pass in this section of the exam; it is not intended to imply that candidates should replicate the musical ideas in this example track in their exam performance.

Mid-tempo rock

● CD track 15

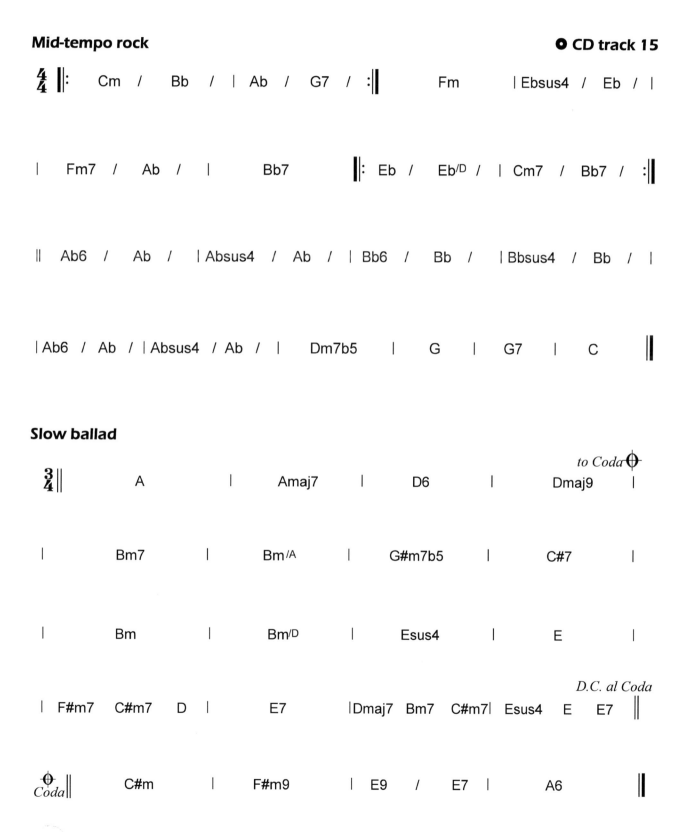

Slow ballad

Uptempo funk

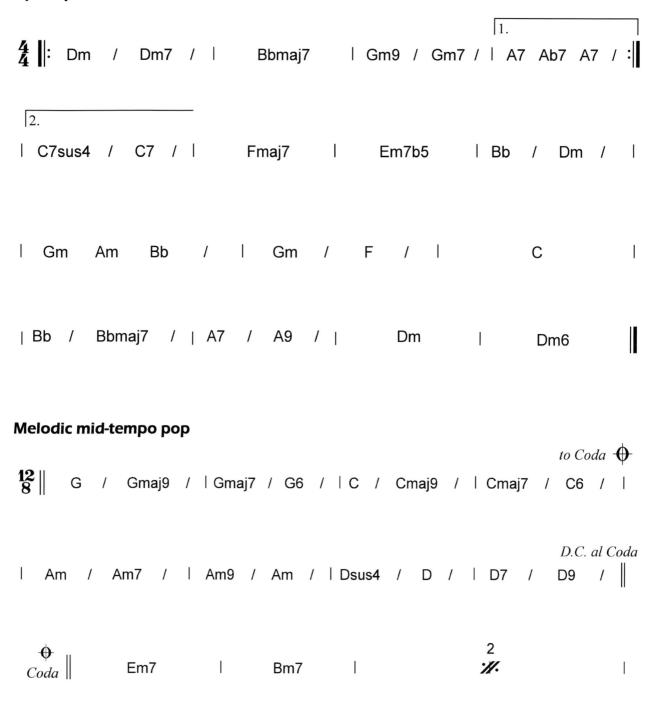

Melodic mid-tempo pop

Please note that the chord progressions above are supplied purely to provide examples of the *type* of chord progression that may occur in the exam. The above examples are NOT the actual chord progressions that candidates will be presented with in the exam.

During your performance you are expected to be able to interpret the following repeat signs that may be included on the chord chart:

Repeat dots

Passages to be repeated are indicated by two vertical dots at the start and end of the section to be repeated. For example:

$\|\colon$ A | D $\colon\|$ A | E $\|$

should be played as :

$\|$ A | D | A | D | A | E $\|$

D.C. (Da Capo – from the head) means play again from the beginning.

Al Coda (to the tail) means play the end section. This is marked with a coda sign ($\oplus$).

/.   Repeat the previous bar.

//.   Repeat the previous bars (number above the symbol indicates the number of bars to repeat).

1ˢᵗ and 2ⁿᵈ time endings

Bars marked ⌐1.⌐ are included in the first playing but omitted on the repeat

playing and replaced with the bars marked ⌐2.⌐
For example:

Should be played as:

$\|$ A | A | D | E7 | A | A | Bm | C#m $\|$

Performance Tips

Your rhythm performance should be musically and stylistically appropriate to the general style suggested by the title of the chord chart. Whilst you are expected to demonstrate evidence of your own individuality you should also be able to draw upon relevant musical influences to ensure a musically appropriate performance. The title of each chord chart also provides some general indication of the approximate tempo, but with the precise performance tempo being left to the discretion of the candidate.

As you are expected to demonstrate proficiency in a wide range of rhythm playing techniques, your performance will be enhanced by incorporating some of the techniques listed below, where musically appropriate.

- Different fingerboard positions of the same chord: a variety of chord voicings, including the use of open chords, barre chords and partial chords.
- Use of extended or altered chords to embellish the basic chord symbols.
- A range of strumming styles.
- Plectrum and/or fingerpicking arpeggiation.
- Single or double-note licks between chords.
- Splitting chords between bass and treble parts.
- String-damping (both fretting-hand and strumming-hand).

You are required to use a clean rather than distorted sound for this section of the exam. However, any other appropriate guitar effects can be used provided you can set them up promptly and unaided. The examiner will not assist with this and may ask you to proceed with the exam without the use of effects if you are unable to set them up very quickly and efficiently.

Chart Reading

Candidates will be presented with a previously unseen chord chart including a notated rhythm part in $\frac{4}{4}$ time. Candidates are allowed three minutes to study the chart and are then required to play the chords, following the notated rhythm.

The range of chords presented will be restricted to: major; minor; major 7; minor 7; dominant 7; minor 7b5; sus 4; power (5th) chords.

The chord chart will be *predominantly* diatonic, although some non-diatonic chords may be included. The chord progression will be limited to keys generally used in pop and rock music. Some common repeat signs may be included.

In order to obtain a high mark for this section, candidates should demonstrate a consistently secure level of accuracy, fluency, clarity and articulation, in a confident and musical performance featuring effective use of dynamics.

Candidates are at liberty to use either a clean or distorted sound for this section of the exam, provided the overall musical result can be heard clearly.

Example Chord Progressions

The following are examples of the *type* of chord chart candidates may be presented with in this section of the exam. The first example has also been included on the accompanying CD – purely to provide an example of the approximate standard of playing and musicianship that is expected for a pass in this section of the exam.

Moderately   ◉ CD track 16

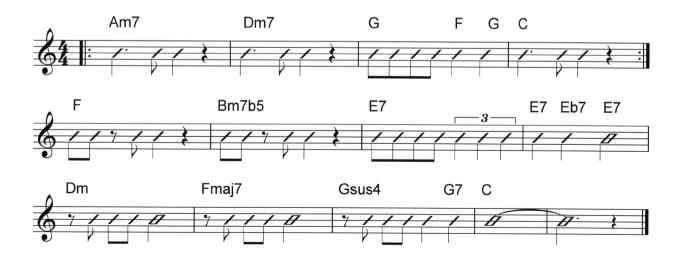

29

Fairly fast

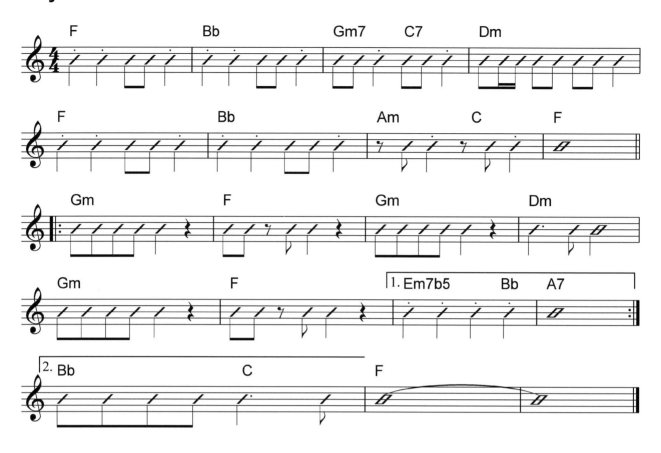

Fast

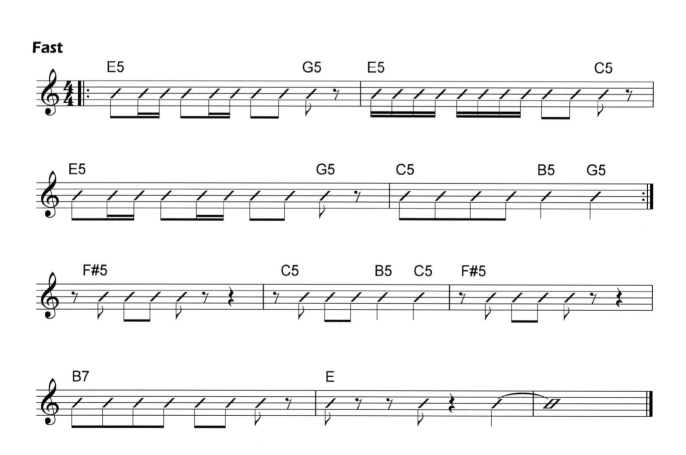

Mid-tempo

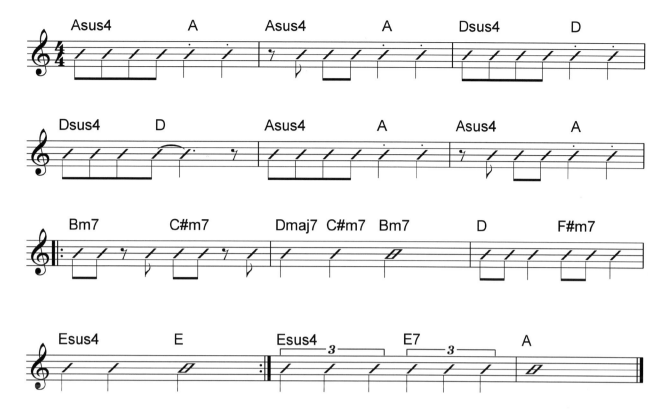

Please note that the chord charts above are supplied purely to provide examples of the *type* of chord chart that may occur in the exam. The above examples are NOT the actual chord charts that candidates will be presented with in the exam.

Performance Tips

- Each chord chart includes a broad indication of tempo, however accuracy, fluency and clarity are more important than speed for its own sake, providing the performance tempo is not unduly laboured.

- You should demonstrate accurate and fluent control over the instrument at all times, in an assured and confident performance.

- You are required to perform the chord chart exactly as indicated in the notation and without any embellishment or variation of the rhythm or harmony.

- In order to encourage candidates to display their creativity, dynamic markings have not been included in the chord charts; the omission of dynamic markings does not imply that dynamic variation should be absent from the performance – you should incorporate musically appropriate dynamic variations into your performance.

Exam Entry

An exam entry form can be downloaded from the RGT website [www.RGT.org], where a current entry fee list can also be viewed. Candidates without internet access should send a large stamped self-addressed envelope, with a short letter requesting a Performance Diploma entry form and fee list, to the RGT office [RGT, Registry Mews, 11-13 Wilton Rd, Bexhill, TN40 1HY]. Non-UK candidates should contact their RGT national representative for information on entry procedures.

Standard Required

Whilst there are no pre-requisite entry qualifications for this diploma and there are no minimum age restrictions, in practice it is highly unlikely that candidates without several years playing experience (including some live performances) will possess the degree of technical ability and musical maturity required for success at Associate level. Candidates should be aware that in this ALCM examination they will be expected to demonstrate a standard of performance beyond that expected at DipLCM level. It is highly recommended that candidates for this ALCM examination study the RGT electric guitar playing grades up to and including Grade 8 level, as well as the DipLCM Performance Diploma, *prior* to entering for this examination.

Marking Scheme

A maximum of 100 marks can be awarded during the exam. The maximum marks available in each section of the exam are shown below.

- Technical Study: 15
- Prepared Performances: 50 [Guitar theme and interpretations 25; Prepared rhythm playing 25]
- Improvisation: 25 [Lead improvisation 12.5; Rhythm improvisation 12.5]
- Chart Reading: 10

Candidates who achieve a total of 75 marks or above will be approved to receive the ALCM Diploma certificate. Those whose mastery results in an award of 85 marks or more will receive the ALCM Diploma 'Upper Level' certificate.

More Information

Candidates should read the Electric Guitar Performance Diploma Exam Syllabus and Exam Information Booklet prior to entering the exam. These can be downloaded from the RGT website: www.RGT.org
Candidates without internet access should send a large stamped self-addressed envelope to the RGT office: RGT, Registry Mews, 11-13 Wilton Rd, Bexhill, TN40 1HY.